Reptile

By Liza Charlesworth

ISBN: 978-1-339-02791-3

Art Director: Tannaz Fassihi; Designer: Tanya Chernyak
Photos © Getty Images and Shutterstock.com.

1 2 3 4 5 6 7 8 9 10   68   32 31 30 29 28 27 26 25 24 23
Printed in Jiaxing, China. First printing, August 2023.

Take a peek at these reptiles!
They are the subject of this book.
It is time to read about them.

croc

skink

A reptile has dry skin and scales.
It can be huge like a croc.
It can be small like a skink.

fangs

shell

spikes

Reptiles have teeth and fangs.
Some have shells on their backs.
Some display spikes. Yikes!

Except for snakes,
reptiles have 4 legs.
They can run away quick.
They can hide beneath rocks.

Some reptiles swim in lakes.
Some bask in the hot sun.
A few stay inside caves.

Some reptiles eat plants and grass.
But lots of them munch on meat,
such as mice, fish, and insects.

Reptiles are so neat!
It's a mistake to dislike them.
In fact, some make fine pets!